More!
Bible Crafts on a Shoestring Budget

Paper Sacks & Cardboard Tubes

An imprint of Hendrickson Publishers Marketing, LLC.
Peabody, Massachusetts
www.HendricksonRose.com

More! Bible Crafts on a Shoestring Budget

Paper Sacks & Cardboard Tubes

Pamela J. Kuhn

More! Bible Crafts on a Shoestring Budget: Paper Sacks & Cardboard Tubes
©2014 by Pamela J. Kuhn

RoseKidz®
An imprint of Hendrickson Publishers Marketing, LLC.
P. O. Box 3473, Peabody
Massachusetts 01961-3473
www.HendricksonRose.com

Register your book at www. HendricksonRose.com/register and receive a free Bible Reference download.

Cover illustrator: Robin Olimb
Interior illustrator: Chuck Galey

ISBN 10: 1-58411-003-1
ISBN 13: 978-1-58411-003-3
RoseKidz® reorder# R38012
RELIGION / Christian Ministry / Children

Table of Contents

Memory Verse Index

Introduction

Do your students enjoy making crafts? No doubt! Next question: Are you looking for crafts that are fun and inexpensive? Bible Crafts on a Shoestring Budget is your answer. Based on everyday items like paper sacks and cardboard tubes, these crafts are designed to get kids excited about the Lord. And with the reproducible patterns and easy instructions, you can focus your energy on teaching the Bible.

Each chapter begins with a Bible story, which is matched with a memory verse and discussion starters. After you tell the story, there are two craft projects that will help students retain the lesson's message and learn the memory verse.

This book is intended to make class time enjoyable for the teacher, too. Each craft includes:

What You Need: a materials list

Before Class: ideas for pre-craft preparation

What to Do: a step-by-step guide to completing the craft

What to Say: talking points to help you relate the lesson

Adapt these lessons to fit your Sunday school or vacation Bible school students. Use them in your Christian day school art classes or in your home. You will be reinforcing Scripture and stories from the Bible — the greatest book ever written — and creatively making a permanent impression on the hearts of your children.

Obedience

Memory Verse

Now go; I will help you…and…teach you. ~**Exodus 4:12**

Now go; I will help you speak & will teach you what to say

But, But, But

Based on Exodus 3:11-4:9

Moses lived with his wife, Zipporah, in Midian. Moses worked for his father-in-law Jethro, a priest in Midian. He took care of Jethro's sheep.

One day Moses was taking care of Jethro's sheep. They were quietly grazing far into the desert. Something caught Moses' attention out of the corner of his eye. Quickly turning, he saw a bush on fire. As Moses watched, he saw that although the bush was burning, the fire did not spread and the bush did not burn up.

Then Moses heard the voice of God coming out of the bush. "Moses, stay where you are and take off your sandals. You are standing on holy ground."

Moses fell to the ground, covering his eyes because he was afraid to look at God. With his sandals off and his head bowed, he listened to God's voice.

"I have seen My people suffer in Egypt. The Egyptians treat them cruelly, forcing them to work hard and beating them if they do not. I will free them from their slavery and give them the land I promised Abraham and Isaac. Go, Moses, lead My people out of Egypt."

"But, God, who am I that I can tell Pharaoh to let our people go?" asked Moses.

"I will be with you," answered God. "Tell Pharaoh that I have sent you."

"But, God," Moses said again, "how will they believe that I am from You?"

God answered Moses' question with one of His own. "What is that in your hand, Moses?"

"It's my staff, God."

"Throw it on the ground," God commanded him.

When Moses threw down his staff, it instantly became a snake writhing on the ground. While Moses stared in amazement, God said, "Pick it up by the tail."

Moses picked up the snake and it turned back into his staff. Moses wasn't done with his excuses, though. "But God, I am slow of speech. I stutter, and it is hard for me to get my words out."

"Then take your brother Aaron with you to speak for you. I think you've given enough excuses, Moses. Now go, and do what I have told you, and I will be with you."

Moses bowed his head. He was the man God had chosen for this job. He would do it to the best of his God-given ability.

For Discussion

1. What do you say when you are asked to participate in a church program or service?

2. Do you have excuses ready to use? Or are you obedient to do what is asked?

Excuse Garbage Truck

Your students will learn that excuses are garbage that needs to be dumped when they make this fun craft.

What You Need

⇨ truck, wheels and verse trash bag patterns from pages 13 and 14
⇨ paper slips
⇨ paper grocery sacks
⇨ crayons
⇨ glue
⇨ scissors
⇨ hole punch
⇨ yarn
⇨ tape

Before Class

Duplicate the truck, wheels and verse trash bags from pages 13 and 14 for each child. Cut the grocery sacks into 12"x18" sheets, one per child. Make a sample truck to use in teaching about excuses.

What To Do

1. Ask, "What are some excuses you make when asked to do a favor?" Have the students write their excuses on slips of paper. Ask, "Do you think God is pleased with our excuses? When we get junk mail we put it in the trash. Excuses are junk, too. Let's put our excuses in this trash truck and get rid of them." Place the children's slips in your truck. Then teach the kids how to make one.
2. Give each child a truck, wheels and verse trash bags to color and cut out.
3. Instruct the children to fold the grocery sack sheets in half.
4. Assist in stapling the two sides together to form an envelope. Cover the staples with tape to avoid injury.
5. Instruct the children to glue the truck to the envelope. Allow them to glue the wheels to the truck.
6. Assist the children in punching holes in each side of the top of the envelope. Tie yarn to the holes for a hanger.
7. Instruct the children to turn the trash bags upside-down. When you say, "Go," the students should race to see who can get the verse together first. When finished playing with the verse, the children can store the trash bags in the trash truck.

SAY

God asked Moses to do an important favor for Him, but Moses made excuses. Finally God told Moses to just be quiet. If you're asked to do something, remember our memory verse. Just like God helped Moses, He will help you, too. Be obedient!

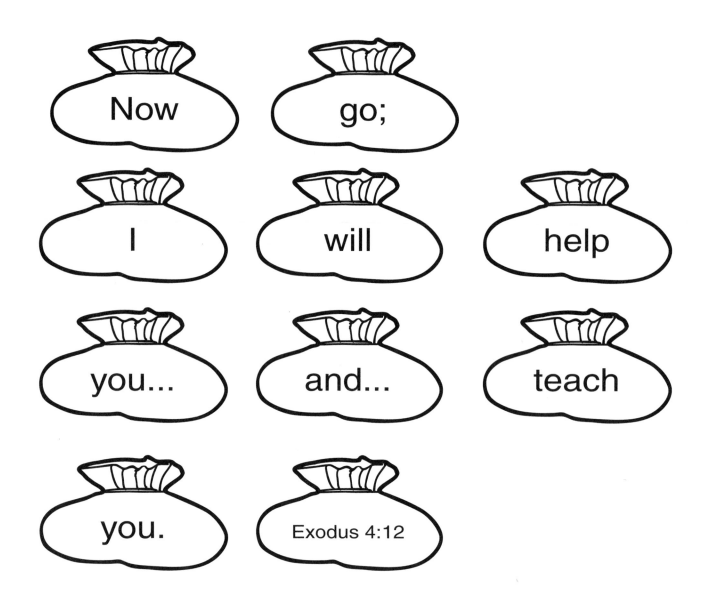

Moses' Maze

The children will use their own creativity to draw a maze where Moses' way will be blocked with excuses until he finally obeys God.

What You Need

⇨ Moses and Egypt road sign from page 16

⇨ paper grocery sacks

⇨ markers

⇨ scissors

⇨ glue

Before Class

Duplicate Moses and the Egypt road sign from page 16 for each child. Cut the paper sacks into 12" squares, one per child. Make a sample maze so the children will understand your directions.

What To Do

1. Give each child a Moses and an Egypt road sign to color and cut out.

2. Instruct the children to draw a maze on the sack square. They should include several "road blocks" where the maze does not continue.

3. At the "road blocks" of the maze, instruct the children to draw or write excuses Moses used for not confronting Pharaoh.

4. Allow the children to glue Moses at the beginning of the maze and the Egypt sign at the finish.

5. Have the students exchange mazes and have a friend try to follow the maze.

SAY

Do you ever use excuses when your mother or father asks you to do something? "But I can't carry that." "But my friends don't have to do that." That's being just like Moses with his "But, but, but." Let's quit making excuses and just be obedient to do what we are asked to do by God, our parents and others who look out for us.

Friendship

Memory Verse

A friend loves at all times.

~Proverbs 17:17

We'll Help You
Based on Luke 5:17-26

Eliud lay on his mat thinking of the things that his friends had just told him about a man named Jesus.

"He's been healing the sick everywhere," said Titus. "I heard he healed a leper yesterday."

"And Peter's mother-in-law—remember her, Eliud?" asked Zobar. "She was sick with a fever, yet when Jesus touched her, she immediately got better."

Eliud's eyes grew bright. "Do you think Jesus could heal someone who is paralyzed? Someone who can't move except for his head?"

"I'm sure of it," said Zobar. "And He's in Capernaum, too."

Eliud grew quiet. "I probably couldn't get close to Him. And how could I get there anyway? I guess that wasn't a good idea."

"Sure it was, Eliud," encouraged Zobar. "Titus and I will help you."

"I'll go get Jotham and Ahaz to help us," said Titus, running out of the room.

Each of the friends took a corner of the mat on which Eliud was lying. They carried him through the streets to the house where Jesus was. As soon as Eliud saw the crowd he knew they wouldn't be able to get close to Jesus.

"Don't worry, Eliud," his friends told him. "We're helping you. We'll get you to Jesus."

The friends pushed their way through the crowds to the stairs that went up the side of the house. Up, up, up the stairs they climbed, never complaining about the heavy load.

Eliud watched in amazement as his friends started lifting the tiles and making a hole in the roof. He held his breath as they lowered his mat through the hole in the roof until he was right in front of Jesus.

What would Jesus say? thought Eliud. Was He going to be angry at what his friends did? But when he looked into Jesus' face, Eliud saw only love and care.

Jesus reached out and took Eliud's hand. "You have such special friends, My son. I have forgiven your sins. Stand up, pick up your bed and go home."

Eliud looked at his arms and his legs, then he tried to move them. They were strong — like he had never been paralyzed. "I'm healed," he shouted. Eliud looked up through the hole in the roof where his friends were watching. "I'm healed," he said to them.

Reaching down, Eliud picked up his mat. "Jesus healed me," he said. "Praise the name of Jesus. He has power from God. I can walk again!"

For Discussion

1. Was there ever a time you couldn't do something by yourself and a friend came along to help?

2. Have you ever helped someone who needed a friend?

Friendship Wreath

The children will enjoy making this friendship wreath. It will help them realize how many friends they have.

What You Need

⇨ smiling faces and bow from page 19

⇨ 9" paper plates

⇨ grocery sacks

⇨ scissors

⇨ glue

⇨ markers

Before Class

Duplicate the smiling faces and bow from page 19 onto colored paper. Make a sample craft and hang it on the door of your classroom.

What To Do

1. Help the students cut the center from a paper plate.

2. Have the children cut paper bags into 3" strips.

3. The students should cut out the smiling faces and the bow.

4. Demonstrate how to glue one end of a grocery sack strip to one end of the paper plate ring and wrap the strip around the ring until it is covered. Instruct the children to glue the end down, then continue the process until the whole plate ring has been covered.

5. Allow the students to write the names of their friends on the smiling faces.

6. Show children how to glue the faces to the wreaths, leaving room at the bottom for the bow.

7. Instruct the children to glue the bow to the bottom of the wreath.

SAY

Sometimes we forget how many friends we have. The lame man was blessed to have friends who cared about him. Don't forget to thank God for your friends.

Twirling Friendship Disc

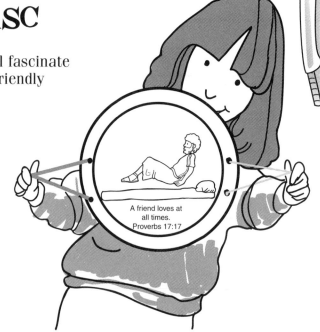

This Twirling Friendship Disc will fascinate your students and remind them to be friendly towards others.

What You Need

⇨ discs and circle pattern from page 21
⇨ paper grocery sacks
⇨ markers
⇨ scissors
⇨ glue
⇨ string
⇨ hole punch

Before Class

Duplicate the discs and circle pattern from page 21 for each student. Make a sample craft to demonstrate to the children how the toy works.

What To Do

1. Give each child the disc patterns to color and cut out.

2. Instruct the children to cut out the circle pattern, trace it twice on a paper sack and cut those out.

3. Instruct the children to glue a picture disc to the top of each circle, then glue the paper sack circles together with the pictures on the outside.

4. Allow the children to punch two holes on each side of the paper sack circle.

5. Assist the children in running strings through the holes.

6. Demonstrate how to hold the ends of the string in your hands, wind the disc up tight and pull. The man will appear to be on his bed!

SAY

Can you imagine what it would be like if you couldn't walk? (Allow time for students' responses.) The lame man's friends did something special for him — they took him to Jesus. How can we take our friends to Jesus? (in prayer)

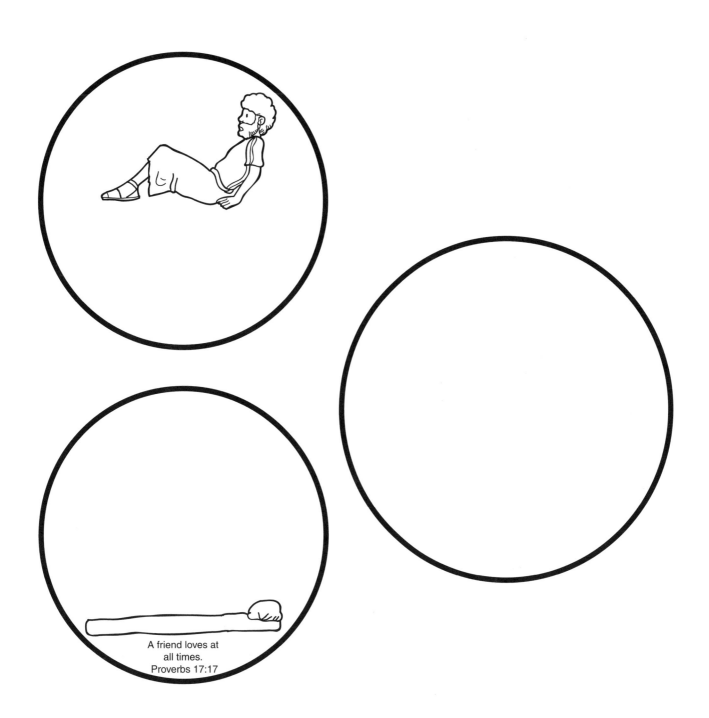

A friend loves at
all times.
Proverbs 17:17

God's Power

Memory Verse

God has the power to help.

~2 Chronicles 25:8

Miracle Cure for Snakebite

Based on Numbers 21:4-8

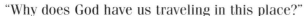

The children of Israel were discouraged. They had traveled and traveled and traveled. They were sick and tired of traveling! As they traveled, they grumbled.

"Why does God have us traveling in this place?"

"I don't know. I wish He'd just allow us to settle down in one place."

"And the food — I'm getting sick of manna."

"Me, too. Oh, for some good old leeks and garlic like we had in Egypt!"

"Or at least some water to gag down the manna."

"Moses should know better, bringing us here."

God was saddened to hear His children grumble and complain so much. He knew there were snakes in the wilderness, but up until now God had kept them away from the Israelites. But because of their grumbling and complaining, God allowed the snakes to roam free. The snakes slithered into the camp and began biting the complainers.

Screams could be heard as first one person, then another was bitten. The poison that the snakes left behind caused an intolerable heat, which felt like fire. It also created a terrible thirst which could not be quenched since there was no water.

A group of people came to Moses, their leader. "Moses, we have sinned against God when we complained about you and God. Pray to God and tell Him we are sorry. Ask Him to take these snakes away from us."

God had Moses make a fiery snake and put it on a pole. The people gathered around to see what he was doing. "This pole can be seen from all parts of our camp. Anyone who gets bit and looks at it shall live."

The children of Israel marveled at the power of God, that He could save them from the poisonous snakes and forgive them for their complaining.

For Discussion

1. What do you think of when you hear, "That has a lot of power"?

2. What kinds of power does God have?

God's Miracles Mural

Working together on this classroom mural will impress upon your students how great God's power really is.

What You Need

- ⇨ verse strips from page 24
- ⇨ paper grocery sacks
- ⇨ markers
- ⇨ glue
- ⇨ scissors

Before Class

Cut apart the grocery sacks and tape them to the wall for the mural. It can be as long as you desire. Duplicate the verse strips from page 24 on colored paper.

What To Do

1. Have earlybirds help you cut out the verse strips and glue them across the top of the mural.

2. Give the children markers and allow them to draw a picture of one of Jesus' miracles on the blank paper.

3. You may want to assign teams to draw a miracle of their choice; or assign miracles so there won't be duplications.

SAY

Can you think of a miracle that you would like to see God perform? (Allow time for student response.) Do you think God still has power to perform miracles today?

GOD

HAS

THE

POWER

TO

HELP.

2 Chronicles 25:8

Snake Pole

Having this Snake Pole at home will remind your students of God's power.

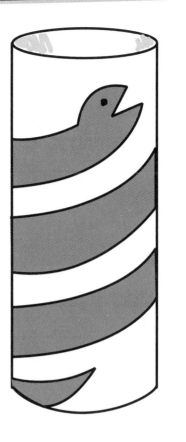

What You Need

⇨ snakes from page 26

⇨ paper towel tubes

⇨ yellow construction paper

⇨ glue

⇨ scissors

⇨ crayons

Before Class

Duplicate the snake from page 26. Make a sample Snake Pole to use in telling the Bible story.

What To Do

1. Give each child a cardboard tube and construction paper. Instruct them to cover the tube with the paper.

2. Allow the children to color and cut out their snakes, being careful to cut the circular solid lines in one piece (have extras on hand).

3. Show how to wrap the snakes around the poles. The tight circular form will stay on the tube without glue.

SAY

God has the power to help us in every situation. It doesn't need to be causing the sun to stand still, bringing down the walls of Jericho or curing someone from a snakebite. Sometimes we just need Him to help us resist temptation or help us recall what we studied for our test. God is powerful!

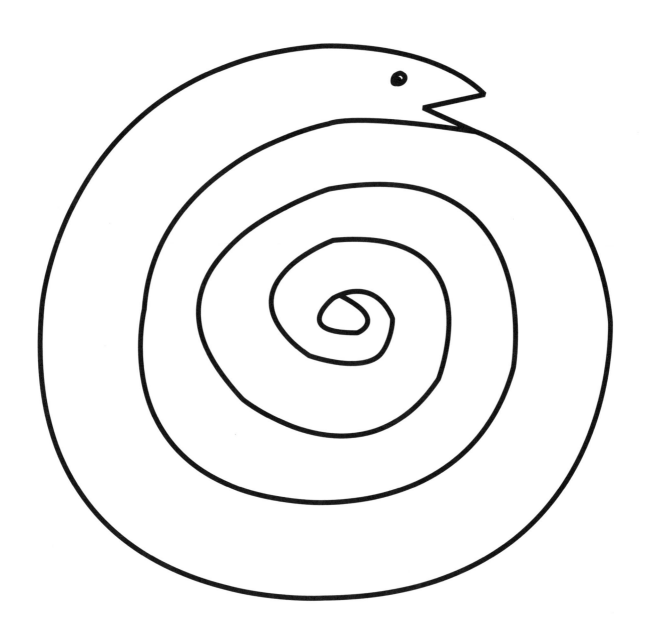

Hope
· · · · · · · · · ·

Memory Verse

Be strong and take heart and wait for the Lord. ~Psalm 27:14

Hurry Up, Jesus
Based on John 11:1-46
· · · · · · · · · · · · · · · · · · · ·

Martha hurried up to Mary. "Mary, did you see Jesus coming?"

Mary wiped her eyes with the corner of the cloth covering her head. "No, sister. He's not coming yet."

Martha's shoulders slumped. "Why doesn't He hurry?" she asked, even though she knew Mary couldn't answer her question. "Lazarus needs Him."

Mary nodded then asked, "Is he any better, Martha?"

"No, Mary. He seems to get weaker every minute. Oh, why doesn't Jesus hurry?" she asked again. "Maybe He didn't receive our message."

But Jesus had received the message. The messenger had said, "Lord, Lazarus, whom You love, is sick."

Jesus was sorry His friend was sick. He had a special plan that would show God's glory to not only Lazarus, but to Lazarus' friends and those who lived in Bethany.

When Jesus came to Bethany, Lazarus had already been dead for four days. He was wrapped in grave clothes and placed in a tomb. As soon as Martha saw Jesus she said, "Jesus, if You had been here my brother wouldn't have died. Why didn't You hurry?"

Mary, too, saw Jesus. "Why didn't You hurry, Jesus? Lazarus wouldn't have died if You were here."

When Jesus saw their grief and the pain they had suffered, He cried. But He knew His way was best. "Move the stone away from the tomb," He commanded.

When the stone was rolled away Jesus prayed. Then He called loudly, "Lazarus, come forth!"

While Mary, Martha and their friends watched in amazement, Lazarus came walking out of the grave, still bound in his grave clothes. "Help him take off the cloths," Jesus said.

Many of those who witnessed this miracle now believed in Jesus. "Jesus," Martha said, "I thought You didn't hurry, but You knew it was best to wait."

"Yes," agreed Mary. "Your timing was just right."

For Discussion

1. Have you ever thought God didn't answer your prayer? Maybe He answered, "Wait." Don't give up, keep hoping…God will show you His power in His perfect time.

2. For what do you need to pray today?

Lazarus' Grave Clothes

This Lazarus craft will remind your students that there is hope in God.

What You Need

⇨ patterns from page 29
⇨ colored poster board
⇨ markers
⇨ paper lunch sacks
⇨ black crayons
⇨ newspapers
⇨ crepe paper strips
⇨ scissors
⇨ glue

Be strong and take heart and wait for the Lord.

Psalm 27:14

Before Class

Duplicate the verse circle and eyes on page 29 to colored poster board for each child. You will need two lunch sacks per student. Make a sample Lazarus. Place it in a large sack and fold down the top. Draw colored question marks on the sack. Before the lesson, ask the children to guess what you have in the mystery bag. Then say, "I'm going to tell a story from the Bible. Listen carefully and you'll see what I have in the mystery bag." When Jesus calls, "Come forth, Lazarus," open the sack and show them Lazarus.

What To Do

1. Have the students cut several crepe paper strips in half lengthwise.
2. Give each student a verse circle and two paper sacks.
3. Instruct the children to crumple newspapers to fill one sack.
4. Demonstrate how to fit the empty sack over the full sack.
6. Allow the children to color the eyes black, cut them out and glue them to the sack.
7. Demonstrate how to wrap the crepe paper around the sack, starting with the end glued at the bottom. They should completely cover the sack, leaving just a small slit for the eyes to show.
8. Allow the children to cut out the verse circle and glue it in the middle of Lazarus.

SAY

Sometimes we get discouraged when God doesn't answer our prayers right away. But we forget that one of God's answers is "Wait." Don't give up. Remember, there is hope!

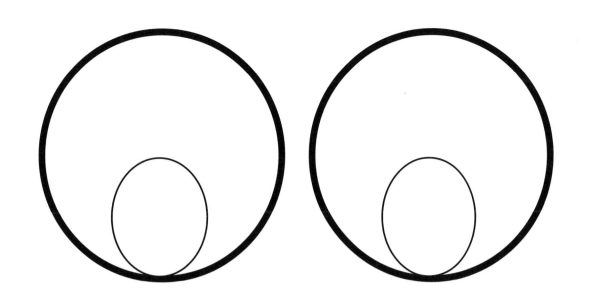

Be strong
and take heart
and wait for
the Lord.

Psalm 27:14

The Waiting Game

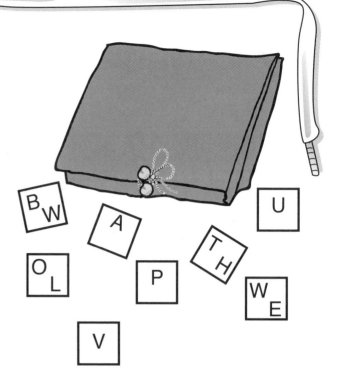

While playing The Waiting Game, your students will be reminded that they should wait for God's perfect time.

What You Need

⇨ patterns on pages 31 and 32
⇨ poster board
⇨ paper grocery sacks
⇨ glue
⇨ scissors
⇨ markers
⇨ paper fasteners
⇨ yarn

Before Class

Duplicate pages 31 and 32 on poster board for each student. Cut grocery sacks into one 8" x 12" piece per student. Make a Waiting Game to show for an example.

What To Do

1. Give each student a pattern page and grocery sack.
2. Show how to fold each piece of grocery sack up 5" from bottom and down 2" from the top.
3. Instruct children to glue the sides of the sack to form an envelope.
4. Allow the children to color the label and cut it out. Instruct the children to glue the label to the front of the envelope.
5. Instruct the children to cut out the letter squares.
6. Demonstrate how to poke the paper fasteners in the envelope. Show how to tie yarn to the top fastener and wind it around the bottom fastener.

To Play

Place all of the letter squares face down on the table. Everyone chooses a letter from his or her pile. If the letter is a W, A, I or T, the player keeps the letter. If not, it is placed to the side. Together, the class chooses letters from their own piles. The first one to spell "wait" stands and says the verse. Other words to spell with the letters are: pray, Lord, hope and love. You can also allow the children to spell two words and the first one to spell either one wins. To play at home, children should keep track of the number of turns it takes to spell "wait." The next game the students should try to beat that number.

SAY

You may find it hard to wait until you get the right letters to spell your word, just like sometimes we find it hard to wait on God's answer. But He knows just when the time is right — and His answer comes just in time.

A	W	D	A	E	I	L
H	I	P	T	L	R	Y
O	P	O	R	D	T	H
V	W	E	Y	V		

A	W	D	A	E	I	L
H	I	P	T	L	R	Y
O	P	O	R	D	T	H
V	W	E	Y	V		

The Waiting Game

Be strong and take ♡
and wait for the Lord.
Psalm 27:14

The Waiting Game

Be strong and take ♡
and wait for the Lord.
Psalm 27:14

Instruction

Memory Verse
Do good…be rich in good deeds…be generous and willing to share.

~1 Timothy 6:18

Letters of Instruction
Based on the Epistles of Timothy

Paul sat on his stool, dipped his reed pen into the black ink and began to write. He was in Ephesus and was writing to the people at the church in Corinth. "Love one another," he wrote to them. "If you have faith that you can move mountains, can speak in many languages, and can predict the future but don't love each other, you don't amount to anything."

Paul wanted the Corinthians to know how important it was to love each other. He gave them other instructions. "Stand firm, dear friends," Paul told them. "Always work hard for God."

While Paul was under arrest in Rome he wrote to the Ephesians. "Be careful how you live. Make the most of every opportunity you have to witness for Jesus. Whatever you do, remember to give thanks to God for all He has done."

He also had instructions for the children. "Children, make sure you obey your parents. You should respect them. This is the first commandment God gave that has a promise. If you honor your parents you will enjoy a long life."

Paul told the Philippians to rejoice. He was in chains in Rome, but was still praising God and instructing others to praise Him, too. "Don't worry about anything," he wrote. "Keep peace in your hearts by thinking on things that are good and right."

Paul loved Timothy and wrote him a letter. "Do your best, Timothy, to work hard, so you will not be ashamed before God. Don't talk about things that aren't necessary. Don't be ashamed to tell others about Jesus."

What loving instruction Paul put in his letters! It was important that they be read and obeyed if those reading them wanted to keep their hearts right with God.

The letters Paul wrote are in the Bible. The words of instruction God gave him for his friends are also good for us today. We need to read them, obey the instructions and rejoice in the obedience.

For Discussion

1. Do you listen carefully when your pastor tells you how to live?

2. Has anyone ever written you a letter with instructions in it?

Mini Mailbox

This miniature mailbox will be fun for your students to make and will remind them to read their mail from God!

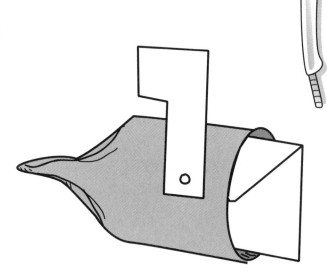

What You Need

⇨ mailbox pieces from page 35

⇨ toilet tissue tubes

⇨ crayons

⇨ scissors

⇨ glue

⇨ paper fasteners

Before Class

Duplicate the mailbox pieces from page 35 for each child. Make a sample mailbox so the students can see the finished project.

What To Do

1. Have the students cut the toilet tissue tubes in half (they will only need one half). Show how to bend the tubes to make a flat bottom.

2. Give each child the mailbox pieces to color and cut out.

3. Instruct the children to write the memory verse on one side.

4. Assist in attaching the flag with a paper fastener on the other side.

5. Have the students glue the lid on the end of the tube, leaving it partly open.

5. Demonstrate how to fold the letter from God like an envelope and put it in the mailbox.

SAY What if you got a letter from your grandmother and you never opened it? You wouldn't know what it said or even if she had put a dollar in it for you to get ice cream. God's Word instructs us but there are treasures in it, too. Read it and find them.

Paul's Mailbag Piñata

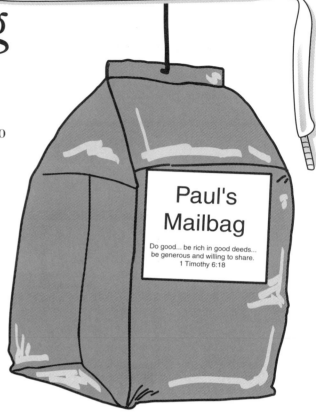

This craft will remind your students of Paul's letters and give them a chance to share with their siblings or friends.

What You Need

- ⇨ bag label from page 37
- ⇨ glue
- ⇨ paper lunch sacks
- ⇨ scissors
- ⇨ large needle and yarn
- ⇨ newspapers
- ⇨ construction paper
- ⇨ candy
- ⇨ stapler
- ⇨ tape

Paul's Mailbag

Do good... be rich in good deeds...
be generous and willing to share.
1 Timothy 6:18

Before Class

Duplicate the bag label from page 37 for each child. Make a sample bag (un-stuffed) to use in reviewing Paul's letters. Write the names of Paul's letters on envelopes (Romans, 1 and 2 Corinthians, Galatians, Ephesians, Philippians, Colossians, 1 and 2 Thessalonians, 1 and 2 Timothy, Titus and Philemon.) Put the envelopes in your mailbag.

What To Do

1. Allow the children to tear newspaper and construction paper into confetti.
2. Instruct the children to cut out and glue the bag label to a lunch bag.
3. Give each child two more bags. Instruct the children to stuff one bag ¾ full with confetti and candy.
4. Have the children put that bag into the second bag. Assist in folding down the tops of both bags and stapling them shut.
5. Show how to put the stuffed bag down in the "mailbag" (the bag with the label glued on it). Assist in turning down the end and stapling it shut. Cover the staples with tape to avoid injury.
6. Using a needle and yarn, make a hanger for the piñata. Try to catch all three bag layers to give the hanger stability.

SAY

Can you name the letters Paul wrote? (Assist the children in naming them). Now we'll see if we were right. (Have them pull an envelope from the bag and read to whom it is addressed.) Our memory verse is from one of Paul's letters. It says, "Be generous and willing to share." Take your piñata home and play the game with your sisters, brothers or friends. Make sure you share!

Paul's Mailbag

Do good... be rich in good deeds...
be generous and willing to share.
1 Timothy 6:18

Paul's Mailbag

Do good... be rich in good deeds...
be generous and willing to share.
1 Timothy 6:18

Peace

Memory Verse
My peace I give you. ~John 14:27

Peace for a Widow
Based on 2 Kings 4:1-7

Elisha was a prophet, a person who travels around preaching to people. Elisha knew that God said in the Ten Commandments, "You shall have no other gods before Me. You shall not make for yourself an idol in the form of anything in heaven above or on the earth beneath." Everywhere Elisha went he tried to make the people stop worshipping false gods. He also told people about God's love. The Holy Spirit was in Elisha helping him to work miracles in God's name.

One day Elisha met a woman, Milcah, whose husband had been God's prophet. The wicked Queen Jezebel had this man, and many other men of God, killed. Women in those days had difficulty making money. Milcah had two small boys she was trying to feed.

"Elisha, Elisha, please help me. I owe money. I have no way to pay it. This man to whom I owe it said he would take my children and sell them as slaves if I don't pay soon. There is fear in my heart."

Elisha stood looking at Milcah without speaking. Then he smiled. "Milcah, what do you have in your house? Do you have anything you could sell to make some money?"

Milcah shook her head. "Just these boys, Elisha. Please don't let them take my boys."

"Nothing else, Milcah?" asked Elisha again.

Milcah thought about her home. "Just a jar of oil."

"Milcah," said Elisha. "Go to all your neighbors and ask for jars. Don't just ask them for one, but get as many as they have. When you come home take your sons in the house and shut the door. Pour the oil from your jar into the jars you have collected."

Milcah knew Elisha was a prophet from God. Obediently, she gathered the jars. When she had all the jars she took her sons in the house and closed the door. Then she started pouring oil.

Milcah's sons watched in amazement as their mother poured oil. She poured and she poured. She filled one jar, two jars, three jars, four jars and still she poured and she poured and she poured. Her jar of oil seemed to have no bottom. Where was all the oil coming from?

"I'm ready for another jar," Milcah told her son.

"They are all full," he told her.

Milcah looked in the oil jar — there was no more oil to pour!

The boys and their mother looked at all the jars in amazement. Milcah ran back to find Elisha. "Elisha, Elisha, I have so many jars of oil I don't know what to do with them all," she said.

"Go and sell the oil. You will have enough to pay the money you owe. You will still have money to spare for you and your sons to live." What peace filled the widow's heart!

Together the boys and Milcah knelt and praised God for providing for the gift of peace.

For Discussion

1. What do you do when the world seems all mixed up and your heart feels uneasy?

2. Who can we ask for peace?

Cup of Peace

This Cup of Peace game is easy to make and play. Each game will remind your students that the same peace the widow had can be theirs, too.

What You Need

⇨ tube wrap, bottom circle and game pieces from page 40

⇨ paper towel tubes

⇨ scissors

⇨ glue

⇨ tape

Before Class

Duplicate the tube wrap, bottom circle and game pieces from page 40 for each child. Cut the tubes into 3" sections, one per child. Make a sample game so you can participate in the game.

What To Do

1. Give each child a tube wrap, bottom circle and game pieces to color and cut out.

2. Have the children cut the bottom circle on the dashed lines as well and form the circle over the end of the tube, then tape it to the tube.

3. Allow the children to glue the tube wrap around the tube.

To play the game:

Put the game pieces in the cup.

Shake the cup and spill the pieces out on the table.

See if you have enough letters to spell PEACE. Question marks can be used for whichever letter you wish.

Put the pieces back into the cup and try again.

The first one to spell PEACE stands up and says the memory verse.

SAY

Who promised to give peace to us? (Jesus) Can we have peace in our hearts if we are worrying about schoolwork, our parents or friends? (no) Give your worries to Jesus and He'll give you peace!

A	A	P	P	E	E	C
?	?	Q	Q	Z	Z	C
T	T	E	E			

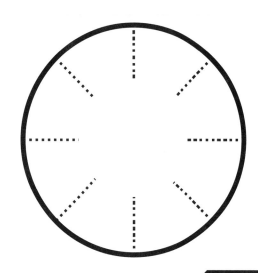

My peace I give you.

John 14:27

Miniature Windsock

Your students will enjoy making this cheerful windsock to remind them of the peace Jesus can give them.

What You Need

⇨ windsock wrap from page 42

⇨ paper towel tubes

⇨ yarn

⇨ scissors

⇨ glue

⇨ markers

⇨ hole punch

Before Class

Duplicate the windsock wrap from page 42 for each child. Provide a variety of yarn colors. Make a sample windsock so the children can see the finished project.

What To Do

1. Give each child a windsock wrap to color and cut out.

2. Instruct the children to glue the wrap to a paper towel tube.

3. Allow the children to punch holes where indicated on the wrap.

4. Assist in tying yarn through the holes. Tie the top two lengths together to form a hanger for the windsock.

SAY

Are you ever afraid of the dark? Do you worry about getting lost? Do you have other worries? (Allow time for discussion.) Tell Jesus what you are worrying about and He will make your heart peaceful.

Praise

Memory Verse
You are worthy, our Lord and God, to receive glory. ~**Revelation 4:11**

I Praise You, Jesus
Based on Acts 12:1-19

"Did you hear?" asked one man.

"Hear what?" another asked.

"That Jesus is coming through here," said the first.

At the words of the man, nine other men suddenly stopped what they were doing to listen. Finally, one spoke. "Jesus is coming, you say?"

These ten men had leprosy, a terrible disease, and they had heard wonderful things about Jesus and His power to heal. Could it be possible that Jesus would heal them? The lepers were filled with hope as they quickly walked as close to the road as they were allowed.

Lepers were not allowed to be near the road where people would be walking because they were afraid of catching the dreaded disease. So when the lepers saw Jesus, they had to call loudly, "Jesus, Jesus, please have mercy on us. Take away our leprosy, Jesus."

Jesus turned and looked at the men. Their capes had hoods that covered their heads. They had scarves around their faces. This was so no one would have to look at their horrible sores.

"Yes," answered Jesus. "I will heal you. Go and show the priests that you are healed of your disease."

The ten men ran quickly toward town. They knew that as soon as the priest saw that they were healed from their leprosy they could go back home.

All of a sudden, one man stopped. Jesus had healed him and he had forgotten to even say, "Thank You." Running back to where Jesus was, he knelt down. "Jesus, thank You. Thank You for healing me," he said. "I will praise Your goodness to all I see."

Jesus looked around. "It pleases me that you are thankful, but where are the others? Didn't I heal ten lepers?"

Only one leper thanked Jesus for healing him. The leper promised to praise Jesus for what He had done for him.

For Discussion

1. Why do we praise God?

2. How often do we praise God?

3. Do we just praise Him out of habit or do we really think about what we are praising Him for?

43

Paper Sack Mat

This "handy" placemat will be a visual reminder to praise God for His blessings.

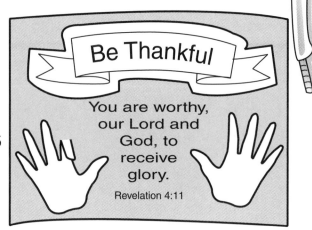

What You Need

⇨ hands and banner from page 45

⇨ paper grocery sacks

⇨ glue

⇨ crayons

⇨ scissors

⇨ clear, self-stick plastic

Before Class

Duplicate the hands and banner from page 45 for each child. Cut the paper sacks into 12" x 14" rectangles. Make a sample place mat so the children can see the finished craft.

What To Do

1. Give each child two hands and a banner to color and cut out.

2. Instruct the children to fold down the finger on the dashed line and glue it into place. This leaves 9 fingers like the 9 lepers.

3. Give each child a paper sack rectangle and show the children where to glue the hands and banner. Write memory verse.

4. Cover with clear, self-stick plastic.

SAY

How many lepers came back to thank Jesus? Jesus asked, "Where are the nine?" When you sit down to eat your meals, don't be like one of the nine. Pattern your life after the one who said, "Thanks."

Poppin' Praise

Your students will enjoy watching the popcorn pop and their plaque will remind them to always be ready to praise the Lord.

What You Need

⇨ patterns from page 47

⇨ construction paper

⇨ electric popcorn popper

⇨ popcorn

⇨ glue

⇨ paper towel tubes

⇨ glue

⇨ markers

Before Class

Duplicate the popcorn popper and popcorn from page 47. Make a sample craft to use in teaching the verse. During class, place the popcorn popper on a sheet in the middle of the floor. Invite the children to sit in a circle around the sheet. Put the popcorn in the popper. When it is ready to pop, remove the lid. Allow the children to enjoy the popping of the corn then say, "Do you notice how quickly the popcorn pops? As soon as it is heated it is ready to pop. We can be like the popcorn. As soon as Jesus answers our prayers we should be ready to praise Him." Hold up the plaque. "Our memory verse tells us that Jesus deserves our praise."

What To Do

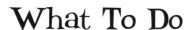

1. Give each child the illustrations of a popcorn popper and popcorn to cut out.

2. Instruct the children to glue the popcorn popper and paper popcorn on construction paper.

3. Have the children write their praises to God on the popcorn.

4. Allow the children to glue the real popped corn around their praises.

5. Instruct the children to glue the top of the plaque to a cardboard tube.

SAY

Like the nine lepers, we may forget to thank God for all He does for us. If we practice praising God immediately, popcorn-style, we'll be like the leper who returned to say thank You to Jesus.

Prayer

Memory Verse
Be...faithful in prayer. ~**Romans 12:12**

Teach Us to Pray
Based on Matthew 6:9-13

Jesus knew He would need people to help Him with His earthly ministry. He chose 12: Simon Peter, Andrew, James, John, Philip, Thomas, Matthew, James the younger, Thaddeus, Simon, Judas and Bartholomew.

As soon as Jesus started performing miracles, crowds followed Him everywhere.

One day, when Jesus came out of the house where He was staying, He saw a great crowd. "Peter," He said, "if I stay here and try to teach the people, only those in the front will hear what I say. Those in the back won't be able to see."

So Jesus and the disciples went to the top of a mountain. The people gathered around on the grass. In the silence of the mountain side the voice of Jesus could be heard by all. It was a colorful sight—everyone in their different colored robes. The poor were there as well as the wealthy. All were waiting to hear what Jesus would say.

Jesus began to speak about real happiness. "Blessed are the meek, for they will inherit the earth." This astonished the crowd. They had always thought the tough would get ahead. They thought those who pushed hardest and were the meanest would be the winners.

It was a sermon on finding happiness. "You should want others to see that you are followers of Jesus and obedient to God. Then you are like a light that is high on a hill for all to see."

Then Peter, who was sitting close to Jesus, said, "Jesus, we see You talking to God, Your Father. Can You tell us how to pray?"

The people leaned closer, they wanted to know what the secret formula for prayer was. Jesus spoke softly, but everyone could still hear.

"When you pray," He said, "this is what you should say:

"Our Father in heaven, hallowed be Your name, Your kingdom come, Your will be done on earth as it is in heaven. Give us today our daily bread. Forgive us our debts, as we also have forgiven our debtors. And lead us not into temptation, but deliver us from the evil one."

Those listening knew what a great prayer Jesus had taught them. First they were to praise God and ask for His will. Next they were to ask God for what they needed. Finally they were to ask forgiveness for wrongs they had done, making sure they had forgiven those who had wronged them. They were to ask God's help in resisting temptation from the devil.

Quietly they began the long trip down off the mountain. They were eager to find a quiet place to put this great pattern for prayer into practice.

For Discussion

1. Do you ever want to pray but think you don't know how?

2. Did you ever wish there was a secret formula for prayer?

Class Prayer Project

Working together on this class project will teach your students the importance of praying for each other.

What You Need

⇨ memory verse from pages 50 and 51

⇨ paper grocery sacks

⇨ construction paper

⇨ scissors

⇨ glue

⇨ markers

Before Class

Cut out or duplicate and cut out the memory verse pieces on pages 50 and 51. Cut the sacks into 5" x 14" pieces.

What To Do

1. Allow the children to assist you in hanging a string in the front of the classroom. Fold the memory verses pieces and hang them over the string.

2. Give each child a sheet of construction paper. Instruct the children to hold their fingers together and trace around their hand.

3. Instruct the children to cut out their hand.

4. Instruct the children to fold a piece of paper sack in half. Allow them to glue the hand on the front of the sack.

5. Instruct the children to write their name on their hand.

6. Allow each child to hang his or her hand on the string.

SAY Look at all the hands hanging up here. Who will try to be faithful in praying for each one of our classmates? Pray that each one will give Jesus his/her heart and live for Him. Don't forget to pray for your teacher!

Be

Faithful

In

Prayer.

Romans
12:12

51

Prayer Cards

Making and presenting these prayer cards will remind your students to "Be faithful in prayer."

What You Need

⇨ praying hands from page 53

⇨ paper grocery sacks

⇨ glue

⇨ scissors

⇨ crayons

⇨ raffia

Before Class

Duplicate the praying hands from page 53 for each child. Cut the paper sacks into one 4" x 6" piece and one 3" x 8" piece per child. Make a sample prayer card and reminder so your students can see you pledge to pray for a member of your church.

What To Do

1. Give each child the two praying hand cards to color and cut out.

2. Discuss for whom the children would like to pledge to pray. Encourage them to each choose someone different. Assist the children in writing the names on each card.

3. Instruct the children to glue the large card to the 4"x 6" piece of paper sack. They keep this one.

4. Instruct the children to fold the 3"x 8" piece of paper sack in half. Allow them to glue the small praying hand card to this piece of construction paper. They give this one.

SAY 5. Help the children tie a bow from raffia and glue it at the bottom of each card.

There are many in our church fellowship who need prayer. Can you think of someone who has been sick? Is there someone who hasn't been able to get out to church? Do you think our pastor needs prayer? What about the janitor who keeps our church clean? (Allow the children to discuss those who need prayer. Offer to deliver the cards to those not able to be in the service.)

_____

is praying
for

_____.

I promise
to pray for

_____.

Humbleness

. . . .

Memory Verse

A man's pride brings him low.

~**Proverbs 29:23**

Look What I Did
Based on Daniel 4:1-37

. . . .

King Nebuchadnezzar was the greatest and most powerful of all the Babylonian kings. Because of this he became a proud man, and had a statue made of solid gold built. The statue was 90 feet high and nine feet wide. It was set up on the plain of Dura. Everyone was commanded to bow down and worship this statue.

King Nebuchadnezzar also fortified the walls to the city of Babylon. "I am the greatest king," he said proudly. "No one can conquer King Nebuchadnezzar's kingdom!"

When the walls were fortified, King Nebuchadnezzar built a new palace, making a beautiful hanging garden.

Still the king wanted to do more. Throughout the kingdom he rebuilt cities or built new ones. He repaired temples and constructed canals and reservoirs, all in a grand style.

"Look at what I have done," King Nebuchadnezzar bragged. "No one before me has built such a beautiful kingdom. I have built this kingdom with my own power and might."

One day, while the king was bragging about his goodness, a voice spoke out of heaven and said, "O King Nebuchadnezzar, you are full of pride. Your kingdom will be taken from you. You will live like an animal, eating grass, until you know that God rules the kingdom of men."

Before an hour was up, the proud King Nebuchadnezzar was in the field with the oxen. He ate grass for his meals, his hair grew long and his fingernails grew like claws. At the end of many years he lifted his face toward heaven and said, "I give praise and honor to the God of heaven. No one on earth is important, only what God says and does."

King Nebuchadnezzar returned to his throne but his praise continued. "I praise the King of heaven. All your works are true and good. You are able to humble the proud."

For Discussion

1. Have you ever heard someone brag and brag and brag, talking only about what they saw, what they did or what they have?

2. How did it make you feel?

3. What did you do about it?

A Puffed-Up Man!

Making and playing with this proud man will reinforce the consequences of pride to your students.

What You Need

⇨ face from page 56

⇨ paper lunch sacks

⇨ newspapers

⇨ stapler

⇨ tape

⇨ beanbags

⇨ scissors

⇨ glue

Before Class

Duplicate the man's face from page 56 for each child. Make a sample man so the children can see the finished craft.

What To Do

1. Give each child a face to cut out and glue to the front of a lunch sack.

2. Instruct the children to crumple the newspapers and stuff them in their sacks.

3. Assist in turning down the top of the sack and stapling. Cover the staple backs with tape to avoid injury.

4. As the children throw beanbags at their proud men, have them race to say the verse before he falls.

SAY Look at the person sitting next to you. Do you think you are better than he or she is? Remember, watch out before you get too puffed up with pride — it will bring you down. Be humble!

King Nebuchadnezzar's Statue

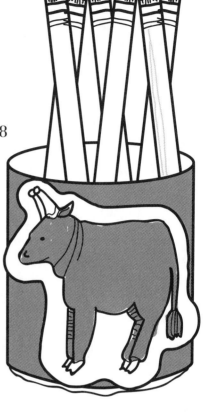

$\mathbf{M}$aking this pen holder will remind your students that pride will bring them low.

What You Need

⇨ statues and bottom circle from page 58

⇨ paper towel tubes

⇨ scissors

⇨ glue

⇨ crayons

⇨ gold glitter

⇨ tape

⇨ paint brushes

Before Class

Duplicate the statue and bottom circle from page 58 for each child. Cut the paper towel tubes into thirds, one third per child. Make a sample pen holder so the students can see the finished craft.

What To Do

1. Give each child a statue and circle to cut out.

2. Instruct the children to cut the circle on the dashed lines.

3. Demonstrate how to fold the cut edges of the circle up the tube and tape in place.

4. Allow the children to color the statue yellow or gold.

5. Instruct the children to paint glue on the statue and sprinkle it with glitter.

6. Allow the children to glue the statue to the tube.

SAY

How would it make you feel to see a statue made to look like you? (Allow time for students to respond.) The king was bragging about how important he was by ordering a statue. What do you brag about? (Allow students to respond.) Why is it important to be humble?

Repentance

Memory Verse

He commands all people everywhere to repent.

~Acts 17:30

Forgive Me, Lord

Based on Acts 17:30

It was a sad day. It was the day for Jesus' crucifixion. Jesus carried His cross along the "way of sorrows" up the rocky hill toward Calvary. He had been beaten until He was weak. When Jesus stumbled beneath the load of His cross, one of the soldiers called, "Hey, Simon, come carry this cross."

Up the hill went the procession. There were those who came to mock Jesus. They were joyous that He was to be crucified. But there were also those who couldn't see where they were walking through the tears that blinded them. There was Jesus' mother, His disciples and those who believed He was the Son of God.

The hill echoed with the pounding of nails as they nailed Jesus to His cross. They also nailed two thieves to their crosses. Then the soldiers sat the crosses upright. Jesus was in the middle with a thief on either side.

The criminal on one side of Jesus read the sign the soldiers had hung at the top of Jesus' cross. "King of the Jews? I've heard about You. Why don't You save Yourself, then save us, too?"

On the other side the criminal said. "Don't talk like that. Why should He save us? We deserve this hanging. We have sinned."

The first thief laughed. "Sure, but if He would save us we could try it again."

"I don't want to try it again," said the other thief. "I'm sorry for what I have done."

Looking up, the thief saw Jesus' kind eyes. In the middle of the pain he saw in Jesus' eyes, he also saw love and compassion. It was enough to give him the courage to say, "Jesus, I'm sorry. Please forgive me."

Suddenly in the midst of his pain the thief felt a joy fill his soul. He heard Jesus say, "This day you will be with Me in heaven."

On the saddest day in history, a thief repented and found forgiveness. He found that no sin is too great for Jesus to forgive, no person so low that He would not stoop to grant forgiveness. Jesus wants to offer forgiveness to all who repent.

For Discussion

1. Are there sins too large for Jesus to forgive?

2. Does He want to forgive us all?

Stained Glass Cross

Your students will enjoy cutting the stained glass for this project. The finished craft can be hung in their rooms to remind them why Jesus died on the cross.

What You Need

⇨ window frames and cross patterns from page 61
⇨ colored poster board
⇨ black and various bright colors of construction paper
⇨ scissors
⇨ glue
⇨ paper grocery sacks
⇨ yarn
⇨ tape
⇨ white crayons

Before Class

Duplicate the window frame on page 61 onto colored poster board for each child. Duplicate the cross pattern on page 61 on regular paper for each child. Make a sample Stained Glass Cross so children can see the finished project.

What To Do

1. Give each child a window frame and cross to cut out.
2. Instruct the children to trace the cross on a sack and cut it out.
3. Allow the children to cut construction paper in small pieces and glue it to a sheet of black construction paper.
4. Instruct the children to glue the prepared construction paper to the back of window frame. Have them cut away the portions of the black paper that extend beyond the frame.
5. Allow the children to glue the cross to the middle of the stained glass window.
6. Help the children make a loop with the yarn and tape it to the back of the window for hanging.
7. Have the children write the memory verse on the back of the black paper with a white crayon.

SAY

Why did Jesus die on the cross? (He died so we could have our sins forgiven.) What is our part of Jesus' death? (We have to tell God we are sorry for our sins and ask Him to forgive us.)

Verse Swag

This verse swag is fun to make, but is also a valuable tool that will remind your students of their need of repentance.

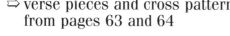

What You Need

⇨ verse pieces and cross pattern from pages 63 and 64

⇨ paper grocery sacks

⇨ hole punch

⇨ scissors

⇨ yarn

⇨ tape

Before Class

Duplicate the verse pieces and cross pattern from pages 63 and 64 for each child. Make a sample swag. Hang it in your classroom to teach the memory verse.

What To Do

1. Give each child the verse pieces and cross pattern to cut out.

2. Instruct the children to trace the cross on the grocery sack three times and cut them out.

3. Allow the children to punch two holes in the top of each piece.

4. Demonstrate how to lace each piece on the yarn.

5. Allow the children to tape the back of each piece to the yarn to prevent sliding.

SAY What did the two thieves who were crucified with Jesus do? (One repented and the other scorned.) Which thief are you like? Are you refusing to repent? Have you repented?

He
Commands

All
People

Everywhere

To
Repent.

Acts
17:3

Salvation

Memory Verse

He saved us...because of his mercy.
~Titus 3:5

What A Change
Based on Acts 9:1-21

Zacchaeus saw a huge group of people. "What's going on here?" he asked. But every one he asked looked the other way. They didn't like Zacchaeus.

"Just ignore him," said one man turning his back. "He's a tax collector."

"Yes," said another. "He collects taxes but charges more so he can keep some for himself."

Zacchaeus shrugged and walked out into the crowd. But he was so short that he was unable to see anything. If only I were taller, he thought. I hate being so short.

Just then he saw a little boy in front of him. Zacchaeus asked, "What's the big crowd for?"

The boy's eyes grew big. "Don't you know? Jesus is coming!"

Zacchaeus had heard about this Jesus. He had heard Jesus was a great teacher and that He could make blind people see, bring dead people back to life and make lame people walk again. He had to see this man. But everywhere Zacchaeus turned there were people, tall people who towered over him. He tried to push through the crowd to get to the front, but as soon as the people saw who it was they pushed him back.

"Go away, Zacchaeus. Jesus won't want to see you anyway."

"That's right, little man. Jesus doesn't like cheaters."

Since he couldn't get through the crowd, Zacchaeus walked over to side of the road. Leaning against a tree, an idea came to him. Straightening up, Zacchaeus gathered his robes around him, and climbed up in the tree. Peering between the leaves he grinned. "Now I can see," he said.

There was a lot of noise in the crowd — some wanted to ask Jesus questions. Others wanted to be healed, and many just wanted to be close to Jesus. Zacchaeus stared in awe at Jesus' kind, patient face. I wish I wasn't such a sinner, he thought. I'd like to talk to Him, too.

Just then Jesus stopped under the tree. Looking up into the tree He said, "Zacchaeus, you'd better get down. I'm coming to your house for a visit and you won't be there if you don't hurry."

Zacchaeus slid down out of the tree as fast as he could. He didn't notice the tear in his robe or the twigs that caught in his beard. He didn't care — Jesus was coming to his house!

That day Zacchaeus told Jesus he was sorry for cheating. "I won't do it again," he vowed. "I will give half of all I have to the poor. And anyone I have cheated I will give back four times the amount that is owed them."

Zacchaeus' life changed the day Jesus came to visit him. And it wasn't long before the whole town knew about it!

"Did you notice how changed Zacchaeus is?" asked one.

"Yes, I did. The change is good," said another who had been cheated. "Isn't Jesus merciful?"

For Discussion

Why does Jesus forgive our sins? Because we pay for it? Because we work extra hard? Because we memorize Scripture?

A Tiny Man

Creating a tiny man will remind your students that regardless of what they look like, God loves them.

What You Need

⇨ pattern from page 67

⇨ paper grocery sacks

⇨ newspaper

⇨ scissors

⇨ markers

⇨ stapler

⇨ tape

Before Class

Duplicate the body from page 67. Make a sample man so the children can see the finished craft.

What To Do

1. Have the students cut four 5" x ½" wide strips from newspaper for arms and legs.

2. Give each student the duplicated pattern to cut out.

3. Instruct the children to trace the body on the paper sack and cut out two. Each child will need two bodies.

4. Allow the children to draw a face on the man.

5. Demonstrate how to staple around the edges of the body, leaving a small opening for stuffing. Show how to crumple newspapers to stuff, then staple the opening closed.

6. Show how to accordion-fold the newspaper strips for arms and legs.

7. Allow the students to staple the arms and legs in place. Have them cover the staples with tape to avoid injury.

8. Have the children write the memory verse on the back.

SAY

Sometimes we think because if we are small we don't matter to God. Maybe you think because your father doesn't have an important job, or you don't do well in school that God doesn't care about you. Put your little man where you can see him. He will remind you that everyone is important to God because everyone can be saved from sins!

Zacchaeus' Tree

The children will enjoy making this stuffed tree, and with it hanging on their door knob at home, it will be a reminder that Jesus saves.

He saved us...because of his mercy.

Titus 3:5

What You Need

⇨ tree and Zacchaeus from page 69
⇨ scissors
⇨ glue
⇨ crayons
⇨ hole punch
⇨ green yarn
⇨ cotton balls
⇨ paper sacks
⇨ tape

Before Class

Duplicate the tree and Zacchaeus on page for each child. Cut the yarn into one 24" length per child. Wrap tape around one end of the yarn. Make a Zacchaeus' Tree so the children can see the finished craft. If you want to use the tree to tell the story, don't glue Zacchaeus until he climbs the tree.

What To Do

1. Have the students cut out the tree top pattern and trace two on a grocery sack, then cut them out.
2. Give each child a Zacchaeus and a whole tree to color and cut out (they don't need to color the top of the tree).
3. Show how to lay the full tree between the two paper sack tops. Assist in punching holes through all three layers about 1" apart around the tree top.
4. Demonstrate how to lace the circles together with the yarn, making sure to leave an opening.
5. Allow the children to stuff the tree with cotton balls.
6. Assist in finishing lacing and tying the ends in a bow. Trim the ends.
7. Allow the children to glue Zacchaeus in the tree.
8. Assist in cutting an 8" piece of yarn and tying it to the top hole for a hanger.

SAY

This tree will hang on your doorknob. What will it remind you of? (Allow time for student response.) Has Jesus saved you? What must you do to be saved? Present the plan of salvation and say, "Would any of you like to be saved?"

He saved us...because of his mercy.

Titus 3:5

Sharing...

Memory Verse

He who is kind to the poor lends to the Lord. ~Proverbs 19:17

You Can't Have It
Based on 1 Samuel 25:2-43

King Saul was a jealous man. He hated David because of his popularity with the people of Saul's kingdom. He plotted to kill David, so David and his men fled into hiding.

While David and his men were wandering about in the desert, they came close to Carmel. This was where Nabal, a very wealthy man, lived. David and his men had to rely on what they could find in the desert to eat. When David realized how close they were to Nabal, he sent several of his men to ask for food.

"Food?" Nabal thundered. "Who is this David that I should give him food? No, you can't have it," he added selfishly.

Nabal's wife, Abigail, who was a kind and very beautiful woman, overheard Nabal turning David's men away. How could he treat them so rudely?, she thought. David has an army of men. They could kill us all.

Quietly and secretly Abigail began loading donkeys with food. By the time she was finished, five donkeys were loaded down with meat, bread, wine, raisins and figs that she had pressed into cakes.

Abigail rode to where David and his men were camped. She knelt in front of David and begged for his forgiveness. "I know we don't deserve your forgiveness," she cried. "My husband was foolish and very wrong for denying you food. I beg you for forgiveness."

David looked down at the woman and felt his heart stir. "Because you have pled for your husband I will forgive you and your selfish husband."

Abigail returned to a sickening sight. Nabal and his friends were having a feast. Nabal was so drunk Abigail couldn't even tell him of her visit with David.

The next morning Abigail told Nabal what she had done. "I was so ashamed of your selfishness," she told her husband.

Nabal stared at Abigail and he became like a stone. He died within 10 days.

David was happy that God had punished the selfishness of Nabal. He sent messengers to Abigail with a proposal of marriage. Abigail agreed to become David's wife.

For Discussion

1. Do you like to share your toys with your friends?

2. How do you feel when someone won't share with you?

Popper Game

This game/craft will be fun for your students while teaching them the fun of sharing.

What You Need

⇨ labels from page 72

⇨ toilet paper tubes

⇨ tissue paper

⇨ scissors

⇨ tape

⇨ ribbon

⇨ crayons

⇨ glue

⇨ candy

⇨ stickers

Before Class

Duplicate the verse label from page 72 for each child. Make a sample craft so the children can see the finished popper. You will use your popper to play the game with your students.

What To Do

1. Give each child a wrapper to color and cut out.

2. Have the children cut a tube in half then stuff each half with candy.

3. Assist the children in holding the two halves together and wrapping them with tissue paper. Show how to tie the ends with ribbon.

4. Instruct the children to glue a label on one side of the popper. Allow children to decorate other side with stickers.

(SAY) To play the game, sit in a circle. Place the poppers in the middle. One child picks a popper and says the first word of the memory verse. That player passes the popper to the next child who says the next word of the verse. Continue around the circle to the end of the verse. The next child stands and says, "Proverbs 19:17," then gives the popper to the next child in the circle who then leaves the circle. Continue until all players have a popper to take home and share.

Sometimes it isn't easy to share. What extra bonus do you receive by sharing with others? (You are being kind to Jesus.) Take your popper home and share it with someone. You will be kind to Jesus!

Share

He who is kind to the poor
lends to the Lord.
Proverbs 19:17

Share

Share

He who is kind to the poor
lends to the Lord.
Proverbs 19:17

Share

Verse Holder

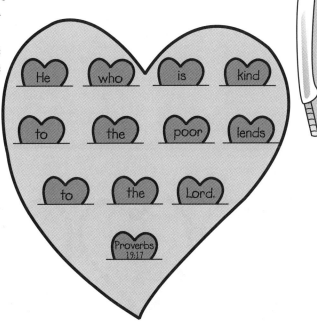

This Verse Holder will encourage your students to hide the memory verse in their hearts.

What You Need

⇨ large and small hearts from pages 74 and 75

⇨ paper grocery sacks

⇨ scissors

⇨ glue

Before Class

Duplicate the hearts from pages 74 and 75 for each child. Make a sample Verse Holder to teach the verse.

What To Do

1. Have the children cut out the large heart then trace and cut out one from red paper and one from a paper sack.

2. Allow the children to glue the large heart to the sack heart along the sides, leaving the top open.

3. Show how to cut 12 slits in the large heart.

4. Have the children trace 12 small hearts on green paper and cut them out. They should write one word from the memory verse on each heart and the reference on the last heart.

5. Instruct the children to turn the verse hearts over and scramble them. At the go signal, the children will see who can put the verse in order first on the large heart.

SAY

Are there times when you find it difficult to share with your friends? When? (Allow time for students to respond.) If you learn this memory verse, you can remind the devil of it when he comes to tempt you to be selfish. God's Word always makes the devil run away!

Thoughtfulness

Memory Verse

Words from a wise man's mouth are gracious, but a fool is consumed by his own lips. ~Ecclesiastes 10:12

Peninnah's Ugly Words

Based on 1 Samuel 1:6-8

Elkanah had two wives, Hannah and Peninnah. Hannah had not been able to have children, but Elkanah loved her more than Peninnah, who gave him many sons and daughters.

Peninnah knew Elkanah loved Hannah more than he did her, and this made her very jealous. Whenever she had a chance, she taunted Hannah about her childlessness. She knew that Hannah wanted to give Elkanah a child and that taunting her about this would hurt her:

"Hannah, you are such a useless wife. I'm surprised Elkanah even looks at you."

"No child yet, Hannah? What good are you to Elkanah? Look at all of the beautiful sons and daughters I have given him."

Hannah said nothing to Peninnah, but often found a quiet place to cry.

Each year the family went to the temple to worship and make sacrifices to God. Elkanah always gave Hannah the biggest portion of meat. His action made Peninnah furious. Again, she taunted her saying, "I can see Elkanah feels sorry for you. Look at how old you are getting, Hannah. You'll never have children."

One year when Peninnah was especially cruel, Hannah left the table before she finished eating. She prayed to God, asking again for a son. "I'll give the son back to You, God, to serve You."

When Eli, the priest, heard her petition he said, "Go in peace, Hannah, and may God grant you your wish."

Soon Hannah did have a son, whom she named Samuel. When he was old enough, she took him back to the temple to serve the Lord. Now Peninnah's taunts no longer hurt. God had given her a son!

For Discussion

1. Although Peninnah's taunting was intended to hurt Hannah, sometimes we are thoughtless and say hurtful things to people without thinking how it will make them feel. Has someone ever taunted you for something you couldn't help? How did it make you feel? What did you do?

2. What does Jesus want us to do in those situations?

Mr. or Mrs. Compliment Puppet

Children will use their creativity to make this puppet, who insists on giving thoughtful compliments!

What You Need

⇨ puppet face from page 78

⇨ paper lunch sacks

⇨ yarn

⇨ ribbon

⇨ markers

⇨ scissors

⇨ glue

⇨ puppet materials (see below)

Before Class

Duplicate the puppet's face from page 78 for each child. Provide any variety of materials for the puppet that you desire. Some ideas: buttons, fabric scraps, yarn (for hair), false eyelashes, wiggle eyes, costume jewelry. Make a sample puppet to use in the activity below.

What To Do

1. Give each child a puppet face to color and cut out.

2. Assist the children in gluing the puppet face to the paper sack. The top portion should go just above the bag flap, and the bottom portion just below it.

3. Allow the children to use the materials to create a unique puppet.

4. Have the students write the memory verse on the back of the puppet.

SAY
Does your heart feel good when you make fun of someone? (Allow time for students' response.) Let's use our puppets to give some thoughtful words to our friends. (Use your own puppet to give each child a compliment, urging your students to do the same.)

Watch Your Mouth

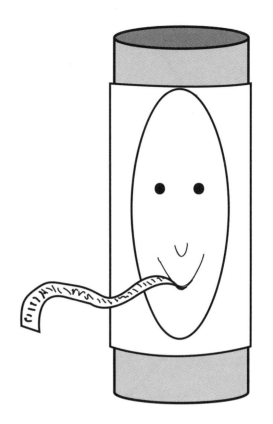

Make this fun craft to remind your students to think before they speak.

What You Need

⇨ tube wraps and verse strip from page 80

⇨ toilet tissue tubes

⇨ crayons

⇨ scissors

⇨ glue

⇨ wiggle eyes

Before Class

Duplicate the tube wrap and verse strip from page 80. Make a sample craft so the students can see the finished project.

What To Do

1. Give each child a tube wrap and verse strip to color and cut out.

2. Instruct the children to glue the wrap to the tube.

3. Allow the students to glue wiggle eyes to the eyes.

4. Help the children cut a slit in the mouth into the center of the tube.

5. Show how to thread the strip up inside of the tube and through the mouth slit.

6. Allow the children to say the verse as they pull the words out of the mouth.

SAY It's up to you what kind of words come out of your mouth. You can't control other's words, but you can control yours. Make them sweet instead of sour.

Words from a wise man's mouth are gracious, but a fool is consumed by his own lips. Ecclesiastes 10:12

Persistence

Memory Verse

Blessed is the man who perseveres under trial. ~**James 1:12**

Go Ahead and Do It

Based on Matthew 4:1-11

Jesus spent His childhood in His father's carpenter shop. While Jesus was growing up, John the Baptist, Jesus' cousin, prepared people for Him. "Get ready," he preached. "There is One coming who is the Son of God."

One day after He was an adult Jesus came to where John was baptizing those who believed. "John, I want you to baptize Me," said Jesus.

John knew that Jesus, although He was his cousin, was truly the Son of God. "I'm not worthy, Jesus."

But John obeyed and baptized Jesus. After He was baptized, Jesus went to the desert to pray. Jesus knew He would be facing hard times in His earthly ministry. He wanted God's help. During this time Jesus didn't eat or drink because He didn't want anything to distract Him from His communion with God.

After 40 days, the devil came to Jesus in the desert. The devil didn't like the plans God had for Jesus. He was going to do everything he could to stop the plans that would save sinners. The devil thought if he could get Jesus to use His power in the wrong way, then Jesus wouldn't be a sinless man and couldn't be sacrificed for the sins of the world.

"Jesus," tempted the devil. "You must be hungry. If You are the Son of God, You could turn these stones into bread." The devil laughed his evil laugh. "Go ahead and do it, Jesus."

Jesus answered the devil quietly. "Having a full stomach isn't the most important thing in life. It is more important to stay close to God and obey Him."

The devil wasn't very happy, but he led Jesus to the top of a high place. They could see all the kingdoms of the world. "Look at all that," said the devil. "If You bow down and worship me, all You see will be Yours." He laughed and said, "Go ahead and do it."

Again, Jesus answered the devil quietly but persistently. "I only bow down and worship the true God, my Father."

By this time the devil was getting angry. He led Jesus to Jerusalem, up to the high point of the temple roof. "Jump off this roof," he commanded. "After all, if you are really the Son of God, He will send angels to catch You." Laughing, he said, "Go ahead and do it."

Jesus spoke again, quietly but firmly. "I will not test My Father, God. Go away. I will not do this or anything else you want. I will only obey God."

The devil left. Jesus was exhausted. God was pleased with His Son for being persistent and resisting the temptation of the devil. He sent angels to care for Jesus.

For Discussion

Has someone ever wanted you to do something you knew was wrong? "Come on," he or she probably urged, "go ahead and do it." What do you say or do?

Angel Bread Basket

This fun craft will help your students remember to be persistent as they resist temptation.

What You Need

➪ verse handle and angels from page 83

➪ paper lunch sacks

➪ crayons

➪ scissors

➪ glue

➪ glitter

Before Class

Duplicate the verse handle and angels from page 83 for each child. Make a sample basket so the children can see the finished project.

What To Do

1. Show how to cut 3" off the top of a paper sack and make a double 2" fold at the top of the sack.

2. Give each child a verse handle and angels to color and cut out.

3. Assist the children in outlining the angel wings with glue and sprinkling them with glitter.

4. Instruct the children to glue the handle to the sack.

5. Instruct the children to glue an angel over each end of the handle.

SAY

What do you think the angels brought to minister to Jesus? (food, water, love) Follow Jesus' example this week and practice persistence. Say no to the devil! Use your basket to be an angel and try bringing something that shows Jesus' love to someone this week. What will you bring?

Blessed is the man who perseveres under trial.
James 1:12

Angel Napkin Rings

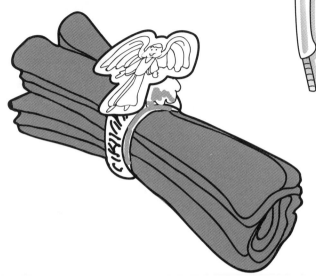

U sing these napkin rings for a meal will be a great home discussion starter for your students.

What You Need

⇨ napkin ring strips and angels from page 85

⇨ paper towel tubes

⇨ scissors

⇨ glue

⇨ crayons

⇨ cotton balls

⇨ paper napkins

Before Class

Duplicate the napkin ring strips and angels from page 85 on colored paper for each child. Cut the paper towel tubes into 2½" pieces.

What To Do

1. Give each student a set of napkin ring strips to cut out (one strip for each member in their family).

2. Allow the children to color and cut out an angel for each ring.

3. Show how to glue the strip around the paper towel tube.

4. Demonstrate how to pull the cotton ball apart to make it larger.

5. Instruct the children to glue the cotton ball to the ring and glue the angel on top.

6. Give the students a napkin for each of their holders and show how to fit them inside the holders.

SAY

Won't it be fun to take these napkin rings home to use for your meal tonight? Take a few minutes to tell your family about Jesus being tempted. Make sure you tell them that Jesus was persistent as He resisted temptation. We should all be persistent and choose to live God's way even when it is not the easiest choice.

Resist Temptation

Resist Temptation

Resist Temptation

Witnessing

I Have Good News for You
Based on John 20:1-18

The day Jesus was nailed to the cross was a sad day for Jesus' disciples and friends.

"How could they do this to Jesus?" asked Andrew.

James shook his head as tears ran down his cheeks. "And to think that it was one of our own who betrayed Him," he said.

They heard Jesus cry out, "It is finished." Then they heard a great rumble and they could feel the earth shake. The sky grew dark as if it, too, was sad that Jesus had died.

The disciples watched as the soldiers put Jesus in a tomb, rolled the stone in front of the door and sealed the opening. They noticed the soldiers who were on duty to guard the tomb.

"Come," said Philip. "Let's go home. We can come back tomorrow."

With slow, heavy steps, the disciples made their way home.

Early Sunday morning when everything in Jerusalem was dark and still, Mary Magdalene and Mary went back to Jesus' tomb to place spices there.

"Do you think the soldiers will roll the stone away so we can put these beside Jesus' body?" asked Mary Magdalene.

Mary started to say, "I don't know," when she saw that the stone was already rolled away. Sitting on the stone was an angel with a shining face and glistening white robes.

"Don't be afraid," said the angel when he saw them. "Jesus is not here. He has risen from the dead. Come in the tomb and see where He was lying. Then go and tell the disciples you have good news."

Turning and running back the way they had come, they shouted, "Oh, Jesus is alive! Jesus is alive!"

Before they found the disciples, they saw Jesus. Joy filled their hearts and bubbled over as they bowed down and worshipped Him.

"Go," Jesus said. "Tell the disciples they can see Me in Galilee."

The women obeyed, running on with the good news.

"John, I have good news for you!" said Mary Magdalene. "I have seen the Lord."

It was good news! Because Jesus died and rose again, we all can be saved.

For Discussion

1. Did you ever see something about which you couldn't wait to tell someone?

2. What happened?

Good News Holder

This Good News Holder will be a great tool to encourage your students to witness to others.

What You Need

⇨ label, verse and cards from page 88

⇨ paper lunch sacks

⇨ markers

⇨ scissors

⇨ glue

Before Class

Duplicate the Good News label, verse and witness cards from page 88 for each child. Make a sample Good News Holder so children can see the finished craft.

What To Do

1. Give each student a label, verse and cards to color and cut out.

2. Leaving the bag unopened, show how to trace the two sides of the label on the front of the paper sacks, leaving a 3" base. Cut in from the sides of the bag to the label, cutting around the label and the other side.

3. Instruct the children to glue the label and verse to the lunch sack.

4. Instruct the children to glue the bag tips together.

5. Allow the children to put the witness cards into the sack.

SAY

These cards are a good way to help you witness. You can give one to the gas station attendant when your parents stop to fill up the gas tank, give one to your newspaper deliverer or to a friend at school. Can you think of others whom you can witness to? (Allow time for student response.) Tell the Good News to others!

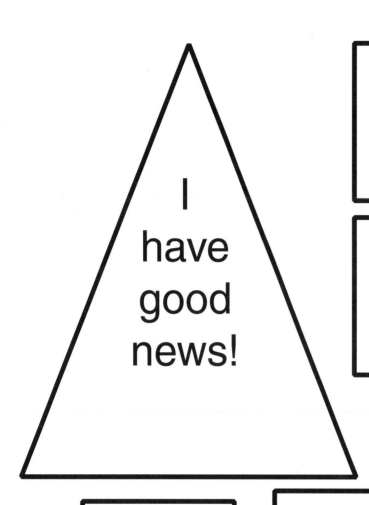

I
have
good
news!

I have good news!
Jesus ♡ U

Ask for forgiveness for sins
Believe Jesus
Confess

I have good news!
Jesus ♡ U

Ask for forgiveness for sins
Believe Jesus
Confess

I have good news!
Jesus ♡ U
Ask for forgiveness for sins.
Believe Jesus
Confess

I have
seen the Lord!

John 20:18

I have good news!
Jesus ♡ U

Ask for forgiveness for sins
Believe Jesus
Confess

I have good news!
Jesus ♡ U

Ask for forgiveness for sins
Believe Jesus
Confess

Witnessing Binoculars

Your students will enjoy reviewing the memory verse with these Witnessing Binoculars.

What You Need

⇨ verse pattern from page 90

⇨ toilet tissue tubes

⇨ markers

⇨ stickers

⇨ glue

⇨ scissors

⇨ rubber bands

⇨ hole punch

⇨ yarn

Before Class

Duplicate the verse from page 90 for each child. Make a set of binoculars so the children can see the finished craft.

What To Do

1. Give each child two toilet tissue tubes to decorate with stickers and markers.

2. Assist the children in securing the tubes together with rubber bands.

3. Allow the students to punch a hole in the opposite sides of the binoculars and tie yarn through.

4. Give each child a verse to cut out. Instruct them to glue the verse to the top of the binoculars.

5. Have the children wear the binoculars and practice lifting them together and saying, "I have seen the Lord."

SAY

What can you see when you look through your binoculars? Allow time for answers. When you see something, you want to tell someone, don't you? When you ask Jesus into your heart it's natural to want to tell someone. Who will you tell about Jesus this week?

I have
seen the Lord!

John 20:18

I have
seen the Lord!

John 20:18

I have
seen the Lord!

John 20:18

I have
seen the Lord!

John 20:18

I have
seen the Lord!

John 20:18

I have
seen the Lord!

John 20:18

Worship

Memory Verse

Come, let us bow down in worship, let us kneel before the Lord. ~Psalm 95:6

Baby Jesus Is Worshipped
Based on Matthew 2:1-11

A baby had been born — a special baby. This baby was the Son of God. He should have been born in the finest home, dressed in the finest, softest clothes and laid in a downy bed made of smooth wood. Instead, this baby, Jesus, was born in a stable where animals were kept. His clothes were long strips of cloth called "swaddling" clothes. And His bed was a manger made of rough wood — not a bed at all but a place for animals to feed.

But His home, His clothes and His bed did not change the fact that Jesus was the Son of God. When Jesus was born, God put a special star in the sky. There were wise men in the east who saw the star and knew that the King of the Jews had been born. It didn't take long for them to get their camels ready and make the long journey to Jesus. They followed the star.

Mary was surprised to hear noises outside where they were staying. Peering out she saw camels. And men dressed in beautiful robes. They were coming to the door!

One of the men spoke. "Where is this baby who was born?" he asked. "We have seen His star in the east and have come to worship Him."

Mary pointed to where Jesus was sleeping. As soon as the wise men saw Jesus they kept their eyes on Him. Nothing drew their attention away from the One they came to worship, not the loud blasts the camels made as they blew air through their nostrils or the presence of Mary and Joseph.

Then the wise men gave gifts to Mary. Mary was pleased with the gifts of gold, frankincense and myrrh. They were gifts fit for a king. "With these gifts we praise this King whom we worship," one of the wise men said to Joseph.

The wise men left, hearts full of joy, because of their time of worship.

For Discussion

1. When we come to church, we should give our full attention to God. Do you think about God, who He is and what He does, and give Him your praise? Or do you think about the game next week or your homework that isn't done?

2. This week at church, try to focus your thoughts on Jesus. He has special things for you to learn.

Baby Jesus Quilt Block

Putting together this quilt block will reinforce the joy of worship to your students.

What You Need

⇨ quilt pieces from page 93

⇨ paper grocery sacks

⇨ pinking shears

⇨ scissors

⇨ glue

⇨ white felt

⇨ crayons

⇨ thin, black permanent marker

⇨ paper clips

⇨ tape

Before Class

Duplicate the quilt pieces on page 93. Make a sample quilt block so the children can see the finished project. If you have younger children you may want to pre-cut the felt and bag.

What To Do

1. Have the students trace one 8" square on felt and two on a paper sack. Have them cut out the squares using pinking sheers.
2. Show how to sandwich the felt square between the two bag squares and glue them together.
3. Give each child the quilt pieces to color and cut out.
4. Allow the children to glue the quilt pieces to the square.
5. Demonstrate how to make small "stitching" lines around the quilt square with a thin marker.
6. Instruct the children to tape a paper clip to the back of the quilt square for a hanger.

SAY

Just like we put together this quilt block, God put together a beautiful plan of redemption for us. It began with a tiny baby, God's own Son. He was even worshipped as a baby before people saw what He could do! We've seen how He can work in people's lives when they allow Him. Let's worship Him now as our Lord.

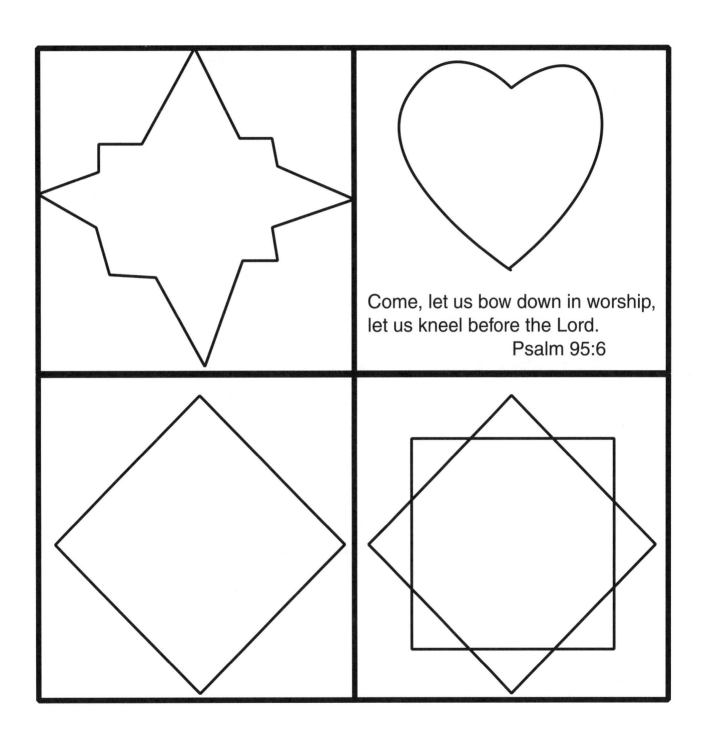

Come, let us bow down in worship,
let us kneel before the Lord.
Psalm 95:6

Paper Bag Church

This Paper Bag Church will be a fun craft for your students and remind them to follow the wise men's example of worship.

What You Need

⇨ church pieces from page 95

⇨ white lunch sacks

⇨ markers

⇨ scissors

⇨ glue

Before Class

Duplicate the church pieces from page 95 for each child. Make a sample church so the children can see the finished project.

What To Do

1. Give each child the church pieces to color and cut out.

2. Assist the children in opening the bags and folding the top down three times.

3. Instruct the children to glue the folded top.

4. Allow the children to glue the church pieces to their bags.

SAY

Where did the wise men travel to worship Jesus? (to a stable in Bethlehem) Do you think we should take time to travel to worship Jesus? (Allow time for discussion.) Let your Paper Bag Church remind you to travel each Sunday for worship. You can even come on a camel if you want to!